BEYOND THE DELIVERY ROOM

KHADIJA HEEGER

modjaji books

First published by Modjaji Books (Pty) Ltd in 2013
PO Box 385, Athlone, 7760, Cape Town, South Africa
www.modjajibooks.co.za

Cover artwork by Megan Ross
Book and Cover Design by Megan Ross
Editor: Rustum Kozain

ISBN: 978 -1-920397-36-4

Set in Garamond

I'd like to dedicate this to my parents Alfred and Elizabeth Heeger, my children, Bjorn, Nicole, Alfred, Wayne and my granddaughter Reese.

The entire book would be taken up by names alone if I had acknowledged everyone here. Suffice to say there have been many, many who contributed to my life and therefore this collection.
Thank you.

CONTENTS

"You, you are the miracle... Yes You... remember how your mother held you? Like that... a stream rushing giddy across pebbles, a harp song holy... Pain makes you forget... We're in this love together..."
Gershwin Wanneburg 2013

Skin matters

I am captive in a mish-mesh of skin
tightened
held together by the infirmities of skin intellect,
skin wit, skin talk, skin designation, skin fragmentation
skin degeneration.
I am bound in the hue that makes you carve for me
a personality, a mind, a heart, a disposition
borne out of skin matters
skin deep.

My mouth explodes into justification, explanation, expletives
to remedy my taxonomy.
I cannot speak,
my voice remains stuck
still choking on that designation, classification,
still finding as I sift through the debris more and more
and more of me
sore and so angry,
so much more of me to free
from skin tyranny.

I have swallowed my words, swallowed my heart,
swallowed my hunger.
I have swallowed my tongue and my blood and my love
to make you safe in your autonomy.
I am captive in the mish-mesh of your mind
sweating through the walls of your fear.
I will not live
here.

Quicksand

In all of this talk of culture and mother tongue
And rich hues of dark mahoganies, cherry, mocha java
and yellows,
in all of this talk of heritage
and identifying who we resemble and what rituals we follow
of locating and relocating the seeds of our beginnings,
whose child am I?
Whose seed becomes me
when I am measured still by the colour of my skin?
And those not knowing where I begin, begin for me a beginning
in their minds,
a beginning I have never known.

In all of this talk of culture and mother tongue
and rich hues blending threads of dark from the night sky
into skin
whose child am I? Where is my place?
I being not black or white, not Griqua or Hottentot or Khoi
or Sotho or Zulu or Venda or...
I do not see these faces in my mirror
and the face I do see
I cannot recognise inside of me.

In all of this talk and talk and talk
of blacks and whites and browns
superfluous themes that fracture me
and you,
whose child am I? Where is my place
and how will you reach me
if you cannot get past the skin
on my face?

Citizen minus

Suffering has a black skin.
How am I to be now that I am made of glass
and words have no sound except for those uttered in a past?
Sometimes I'm black
when politics parodies a truth and quantity is king.
Sometimes I am black.
Sometimes only in the vaguest sense do I have a history
a memory, a cultural reality.
Easier to keep me in the dark,
easier to talk about the Indian Ocean slave trade
as if it were one of the stepsisters,
easier to say that I almost suffered
am almost one thing
not quite another.

Somewhere between here and there
between 1994 and the present
I was lost on the periphery of a South African story
because if memory serves the historical themes it seems
my people were never participants in the resistance
never marched, never fought, never died.

Coloured anomaly
forcibly removed, survivors of slave ancestry
the sum total of my past coined thus
and by degree I'm the not so bad-off progeny.
"We won't omit you completely, we'll just play with the lighting
so it won't look so frightening."
Pieces of a story,
just enough said so you'll go quietly to bed.
Citizen not quite black.

Ek is mos ve'koep dee' my manskap,
'n government wat alwee' praat van equality en freedom
ma hiesie ding: die vinge wys ve'by daa' waa' ek bly,
issie soe bad offie,
maakie saak hoeveel gengsters en drug addic's daa' issie.

It kommie vannie strugglie
and is by definition not defined as an apartheid crime.
Citizen wassie daa' nie, maggie kla nie
vrek van pille roek met 'n apartheid spoek.

And now 18 years later, left with a democratic hangover
and a negotiated new South Africa,
I find that 'not an apartheid crime' ruining the length and breadth
of mostly coloured youth
filling the gap between yesterday and today
with a smell not unlike that of the
underdog.
Unity in diversity becomes a travesty if we omit just one you see
but history it seems is a commodity
something dressed for a particular emphasis
sold to the appropriate buyer.
"But it's not that simple," they tell me, "there are complexities
if you please, don't over-simplify!"
Is it complex to lie, make over, storyboard, edit
till you don't see the ones slipping through the cracks?
Until suffering has one colour and prosperity another?
And I become the pain you see through
now that I am made of glass
and the skeleton of my ancestors can be seen in the faces of the young?

We carve a dubious future at best
but I like a ghost will not rest
until equal means what it is
and recognition is fair
and suffering has no colour;
until I have no more gooseflesh in these modern day prisons of freedom
for all
where we create more underdogs for the next struggle.

Hoekoo' gat o's daa' in 'nni blinddoek vasgevang
gemang dee 'n fucked up understanding of identity?
Hoe vê' aluta, hoe vê' continua?

Ek is mos ve'koep dee' my manskap,
'n government wat alwee' praat van equality en freedom
ma hiesie ding: die vinge wys ve'by daa' waa' ek bly,
issie soe bad offie, maakie saak
hoeveel gengsters en drug addic's daa' issie.
It kommie vannie strugglie
and is by definition not defined as an apartheid crime.
Citizen wassie daa' nie, maggie kla nie
vrek van pille roek met 'n apartheid spoek.

Die dood sing

Ek klim in die hoek
geblinddoek.
Ek klim in die grond, aard kind,
stom van verlange vir myself.
Ek klim in die wind,
onskuld en vasberaadenheid.
Hoeveel moet ek betaal vir jou skaam hier in my liggaam?

 Krotoa en Williams, vaal en krombene,
fluister in 'n maan-aand aan jou mure.
Krotoa en Williams twis en betrap,
met so a tong is geheime verklap.
Krotoa en Williams hang aan skrerwe in ons geheue

maar die stem bly wild soos 'n wysvinger,
die stem bly broei soos die dood en dade,
die stem bly mompel in die grond
van ons aarde.

Krotoa, also known as Eva, was a slave woman who lived in the Cape, became an interpreter for the Dutch East India Company and married a wine farmer.
Lydia Williams was a freed slave who lived in District six. Her ancestry was Mozambican.

Displace
(for District six)

Pebbles spill on this shore
jagged lines mixing sediment with and stumble .
Words are strange on this air where I have never heard
and still in these small seconds roots take in the undergrowth
and echoes of the storms and laughter to come
are born in this place.

In this place where colours mix like time
stones are splattered with laughter, church choirs and bilal,
in this place languages exchange words
tangling themselves in the walls, the sidewalks and in hearts.
In this place where colours mix, another culture comes to life
in all these spaces

and long, long after the ships that sought the women folk,
long, long after money had changed hands and things like names were
stolen,
long, long after roots had grown in earth and memory had lifted skirts
and kissed its first love
and I had grown my own long stories of fights and idle chitchat
 across fences of borrowed sugar and wash-house whites,
long, long after gravestones piled themselves above the ground,
long after dreams were dreamed and shattered,
long after they had renamed us and we had shelved our ancestral pain,
the wind she broke sound and split the seamless air whispering again
of things to come and things to mourn.

It was thunder,
at least it sounded like thunder.
It was a stray-dog howl,
at least it sounded like it.
It was my mother, water eye and frozen sob – yes it was
as the words became more than wind
and the whisper became difference and my heart left me for dead
the walls turned their backs and parted
while I let the voice of photographs carry me away and suitcase messages

write me into another day.
It was my daughter free and green growing here like me,
it was her.
It was me white with fedora and mantilla Sunday on the hill,
it was
once, just once.

It was my country,
jungle bush and African burrows
once, just once.
It was lightning,
at least it looked like lightning.
It was the sound of birds screeching hard against the sky,
at least it sounded like it.
It was my father, blood and bone,
it was his gentle, raspy breathing next to me,
no it wasn't!
It was my mother raped and stoned,
my brother, gun in hand, changing into tomorrow
where no one lived but all my sorrow

and still long after heads are full with inferior and other and kill,
masks and saleable memories linger to tell the stories that don't remember
except to make a hero's monarchy without mixed colours

and so pebbles spill on this shore
jagged lines mixing sediment withand stumble.
Words are strange on this air where I have never heard
and still in these small seconds roots take in the undergrowth
and echoes of the storms and laughters to come are born in
Displace

Breaking news

When we look and you find a glitch in the system,
when we feel all the time that there's something missing,
when we turn around and the door's closed,
our belligerence shows
'cause the politician's wearing emperor's clothes.

When we do the 'they',
when we call it black or white or grey,
when the headlines scream another dead child,
another oil slick,
another hard crime, somebody else is doing the time,
quite frankly I think we should all get in line.
When you say your life depends on the other man's outcome,
"Oh there's so much degradation,"
the government's put us in this situation,
"It's a black dream!" you scream,

I've got news for you:
you're here too.

When your sister's raped and your brother's drugged
and you look at it all and say: "We're all headed for a long hard fall."
When you talk of lies
but still don't speak your truth,
when you can't make it to the top and it's always somebody else's fault,
that the ball's dropped,

when your agitation is all you can spare
and your rhetoric has you all in a rage,
when you can't hold yourself after a fall
and you lay down love and pick up arms
and the silence cries
but your lips still don't move
yet in your own living room you're a prophet of doom,

we tick the minutes, spill the seconds
tick the minutes

spill the seconds
talk judgement, economics and acid rain.

We tick the minutes, spill the seconds
talk memory
talk more pain.
We tick the minutes, spills the seconds.
We talk of God.
We talk more, talk more
talk more
we're keeping score.

When we move to Australia
'cause the country's a failure,
when mending the situation calls for a band-aid solution
to put us inline with our constitution,
when you can't understand how 18 years of democracy didn't make it all fit
and you feel the urge to shout get over it
"Get over it!"
as if it's something outside yourself that requires the shift,
remember people, we're all in the same damn lift
going up or down.

We tick the minutes, spill the seconds
tick the minutes, spill the seconds.
Time is a wasting while we're cutting and pasting
and life is elsewhere
here or there?
Outside's a good place to count the cost
when you're running that race from the inside.
It's better than dealing with the feeling of being lost
displaced in your space.

I've got news for you
it doesn't take an apocalypse to mend a century,
it doesn't take blame to alleviate pain.
A simple step to the mirror is all it will take,

a reflection on the reflection is the only way to free the present from hate.

So strap on your seatbelt or put on your parachute,
the ride's scary or sacred, could be heaven's door or hell's gate.
All depends on your internal state
but unless you're late, deceased or carried off in a crate
don't berate the psychosis and add to the neurosis.
Simply take a look in the mirror at your own thriller,
dispense with the polyfilla.

I've got news for you
you're here too.

Under my tongue

A man said to me the other day: "But it's a new democracy,
why are you so angry still?"
I said: "I'm not angry, impassioned maybe, not angry."
Okay, maybe a little.
And just before, just before I was ready to choke on the blame again,
I remembered that his fear was making me feel shame at my anger
and my shame was making me feel anger at the blame.
I thought: "Perhaps I shouldn't talk of these things anymore, close the chapter,
slam this door."
Because after all it's not about race,
though race was used to put me and keep me in my place;
it's ultimately about human dignity,
the right to be.

Yet I couldn't or I wouldn't let go of the undercurrent in that statement
which meant I had no right,
no need, to talk of these things
because my examination would mean his contemplation of his reality.
Still I can't live in his eyes,
those far eyes that hide in words where trembling hates a mirror.
He wanted me to wear that new South African disguise
another mask

but I must talk,
talk hard-talk, soft-talk, talk redfire-talk,
talk cry-talk, stone-talk, water-talk
so I can talk laugh-talk
after things tumble free from under my tongue and deep inside my throat.
I must talk because new South Africa is not enough to disguise the lies
or the slap in my grandmother's face, my sister beside her,
hip-high, cream-coloured
and slant-eyed.
None of them look like me on the outside.
I am like my father's people,
yellow ends and veined palms.

Despite what you may think
on the inside I am like you
plus/minus broken heart for stares they met and lines they couldn't cross,
lines that still shape the breadline
as if money can make it all go away.
Money does make it easier though
to talk like you, eat with you
fill out the repertoire as we now climb over leafy suburb walls,
our scalpels fussing over an edit
to be where people count their black friends
with just the right accents and complexions
to present as little compliments for their benevolence.

Black Label introduction

I have twisted your words,
twisted them into my skin
back and forth, back and forth
like the click-click of a loom.
I have twisted your words
into my hair and my breasts,
twisted them into my tongue and my teeth and my thoughts.
I have platted and woven and burned them into this tapestry
until finally I see there is this image called me.

A collision of disguises in fruitless beginnings converge with time
to crack silences that live beyond the cacophony of this image
and my sound breaks into
to reveal the suddenness of something true.
I am not your words.
I need not answer to those words.

Black label

Somebody killed the music and wrote discord
and told us all to make mad noise and like it
crying about the hole in the bucket
so here we are paying to be lulled by some strange tune.
You can do this at home in our living room
but there's a TV I presume streaming in the sub-human text
filling the decibel quota so your offspring can develop a catatonic stride.
We call it national pride,
everything else is nullified.

Are you up for manipulation?
Can you ask why? Can you ask why
and then look yourself in the eye?
Can you ask why was Bush a president?
Can you ask why was Bin Laden resident?
Can you ask why HIV and internalised oppression
has Africa on its knees?
Can you ask why this has now become a black disease

and look yourself in the eye if you please?
Can you ask why black
why white
why coloured?
Can you ask why we keep the love in the media,
selling ourselves this dilution
afraid of the solution?
Can you ask why
and then look yourself in the eye?

Can you ask why 80% controls 20%
and then ask why your mother can't pay the rent?
Can you ask why your human family is living street-bound?
Can you ask why there's no change?
No change
no change
no change
just some poor fool like me that's up on a stage and complains?
Can you ask why your father shot himself?
Can you ask why the shit's so deep
like the nothing that we speak,
flagrant testimony of that tired scripture
"It's because I'm black you see"?
Can you ask why we keep clamouring to be just like the picture
of whitey?
I'm talking the material economy and how it's used you see
and it just so happens it comes with that pristine mentality
Jik-clean and pristine!
Yet I don't see us taking control of our destiny
I just keep hearing:
What's that you're saying?
"It's because I'm black you see."

Ah but that's the famous copout for the dropout, for the victim
and though it's true
it's still no excuse to think that makes up for exemption
from our own redemption.

Is your life worth a mention
or are we going to live in mimicry
or find a way to see the change
see the change
see the change
in you and me?

Can you say "I am"?
Can you say "I am the"?
Can you say "I am the change, I am the change, I am the change,
I am the change"?

Or are we just ready to toy with the last remains of another idealistic notion
and prepare ourselves to grow old in the economic handout game
because we're just too damn lazy to create humanity differently
without screaming
it's because I'm black you see?!

So let me get this straight:
black means we can't wake up from a struggle mentality and free ourselves
from a victim reality?
Oh my brothers and sisters, what's that you keep saying:
"Hey man it's always been that way"?
When did you give up?
How many times have you been bought and bartered for?
Oh yes, that's right. I forgot there's no slavery anymore.
It's pusillanimity,
voluntary contribution to some more systematic distribution
of bubblegum identity
division precision
and what's more, an abuse of sameness in the name of unity
for the quick march of your own thoughts
to the march of the massive identity,
the one that's not about you or me
getting caught in the PC tradition.
It's getting away with omission,
assume the position.

Possibility is probability,
is likely
is can be
it's just up to me.
Our choice means it could be
should be
a different history.
Wake up from that victim mentality
that's the control
you see.

There is no system we are not a part of,
there is no difference we cannot be the start of.
How we use it is the key
and if it's going to harm the one next to you
you may as well be the gun or the knife
and the hypnosis too
because it doesn't matter what flag you're flying
or what colour you're buying,
if you're marching with a deadly compromise
you're just wearing that disguise, the one that we call
colonised.
Your identity is rooted in the 'me',
the master of your destiny.

Otherwise whose nigger are you?
Nigger is the myopic ass with the power to change,
who assumes his future depends on a handout
to get out
of himself, herself, yourself
myself.
I said get up!
Or get down on all fours and drop drawers.
Now I ask you
does that give the victim in you pause?

Can you say '"change"'?

Can you say, "I am the change, I am the change, I am the change"?
Can you ask why
a question is worth a million assasinations, dissertations,
simulations and virtual realities?
Can we give up this disease?
No more liberation from the outside!
This is an inside story.
This is not about glory or dream making.
It's a simple question of not playing
the shame game.

Africa can you say it?
I am the change
I am the change
I am the change
I am the change
I am
the change!

Pearls and beads

I can't make you care.
Caring is often the benefit of suffering
and real suffering settles in the bones like the words of those you love
then learn to hate.
I can't make you care
that you could never understand the way that Africa winds its beaded brow
and bony, scorched feet each day under the weight of your excess.

I can't make you care
about your apathy or give up your social pedantry in favour of stark self
analysis
or understand that we are not separate nor will we ever be from you who
live there,
we who are beaten down, convinced by ideas about us
till some of us eventually buy those ideas as if they were rare pearls
to be worn in place of coloured beads, forgetting that pearls are just beads
too,
those pearls that sell ideas that birth dying Africa's
cradling monsters like Wallacedene, Manenberg, Langa, Khayelitsha,
now airbrushed township tours for your pleasure
masquerading in the pretense of long, long ago,
those pearls that travel hollow with the stench of swine
and declare themselves with fluent hubris, holier.

With a single sweep of your words you say you see, you understand
but between your lithe first world crap
your lack begins to show.
You bury yourself under the skin of a modern missionary
and bleed through eyes in forced blood some thing like pity,
assuage your guilt with self-righteous indignation: "But I've come to help."
Offer your body to my brothers and sisters as compensation.
I'd sooner you stopped feeling bad so I can get on with my suffering.
I have so few ragged smiles left in my harlot's face for you
and I don't want to spare you anymore the slow burn that issues
from the belly of your history,
your consultation with your ancestry.

And after everything,
all that has gone and stayed in the maze of colonialism and first world
semantics,
still there is this:
the burden of your guilt keeping me in the prison of my suffering,
trapped there between the lush eloquence of this mime of mine
and that excess of yours.

A very new old South Africa

Sssh, be still
eyes closed, tongues quiet.

Sssh silence
under the tepid slogans of a new South Africa.
Sssh here between leaves and vortex hills, we dream the dream of a
rainbow glow
while children grow on plantation townships
amid diamond addictions forged deep in history
and makeshift dreams stagger languidly
bent on lips like dop, sugar sweet honeydew
the new Revlon shade in township trash.

Bondage is a mind gone south for the summer for a township tour
on the lip of Khayelitsha or Manenberg.
Bondage is domestic bliss,
blissful domestics cradling other mother's children while their own play
in streets of corrugated iron and matchbox poverty.
Bondage is a mind living with covered mirrors cuddling up to a cloistered
tongue.
Bondage is the words you will not say hoping you can make me go away.
Bondage is the memory buried deep and the stories you will not hear me
say.
Packed in a suitcase one fine day, 27 April 1994,
I live outside of freedom's door.

Missing,
are you missing me a child of three?
Missing,
are you watching your daughter and your son?
It could be them,
they could be the one, the one of three just like me
missing.
On an ordinary day two years ago my photo stays on the station wall
a hopeless hope, an undug grave, a sniff too long for a sniffer dog,
a blink...
it happened somewhere else

not here, not near, not dear.
Ah, it's a very new old South Africa my children,
a very new old South Africa.

I am gunmetal tragedy
trouble like you won't believe.
War is my mentality.
You grow me up in grim effigy,
I live inside your house and in our home
a picture in a newspaper:
the latest Hollywood blockbuster – removed to a pixellated conscience.
I am best served with popcorn to high-minded folk with trust funds
and United Nations aspirations.
I am that boy, AK47 mind,
a twisted flower on a spineless humanity.
When will you see me?
Your child could be me.

Tomorrow is a children's paradise carved out of smokescreens and mortar.
Tomorrow is a dungeon of old dug deep to hide sins.
Fathers don't speak of such things and mothers cry long before today.
I am at best a theory, a seminar, a doctoral thesis.
I am a signpost in the traffic of everyday things, I am everyday things.
Everyday is where you hide me in coffee for two, soap opera rumours
and the hieroglyphics of amnesia.
"Maps that don't read well," you say.
Which township was that in the news the other day?
It doesn't matter anyway.

We are ghosts you see floating in and out of life.
Conscious is not our preferred drug so we create more ghosts,
motherless children, childless mothers, homeless humans, delinquent
fathers
eloquent liars articulating to a fault mercenary democracy.
We have developed the perfect cataract – an industry of development that
doesn't work.
Township traumas have become the bread and butter of many,

those cheap labour plantations.

But sssh, it's over now
slavery is long gone
apartheid is dead
not a racist in sight, not a victim for miles.
Assimilation is transformation, assimilation is transformation
on the planet of silenced dialogue.

Any other planet but here

(for the victims of Human Trafficking)

This is another planet,
my limbs sawn off like bits of wood
cut up like meat, diced like the gamble of nation on nation
rape, wrong, child, woman, man, level bought, sold, heinous, hard-on,
wounded
underground
where we hide our indignation
banked for an easier cause.

I am another planet.
I am no sound on the airwaves
no taste on a tongue, no memory, no photograph.
I am no name.
No one will ever say my name
catch my ball as it rolls across the lawn.
Here on this planet there are no lawns
no trick-or-treat or Christmas songs sung or New Year's eve kisses to say:
"I love you."

My body is a battlefield in evolution,
the tension that makes mockery of freedom for all.
My body is the alarm bell in the steeple of abolition,
degradation, pieces of a dream.
I am the place where sex becomes sin
and you swallow the moan on my skin.
I am outside
a zillion light years away stretched across faces
spilling onto city streets wiped clean with neon filters
in those star-spangled banners and rainbow-clad colours.
I am the lyrics you do not sing, the march you have not marched,
the victory you have not won.

My body is the planet of things,
the Grand Central Station of modern day slavery,
the ruled-out fact that no one dare utter at Sunday mass
and no government dare emphasise as political fact

like the one that says "Policies are for pussies!"
long drawn out paper towers that hang me.
I am cut up twisted on the verge of death without death
and you look through me.

My body is a counterfeit note in progress,
a proof that we have all lost the ability to scream
our voices gone numb in our throats
while we gorge on freedom slogans and push placard consciences
and believe that in our days of daze
we can feel safe because we didn't know
murder by omission
and we close our eyes yet again and hum another tune
till Jingle Bells begins to ache all around me
taking the Christ out of Christmas
keeping ignorance in the traffic of everyday things.

Whore's paradise

My skin is made of glass.
I am a strumpet who stole words from sentences on your foreign tongue
as we lay encumbered by the missionary.
I made insult in your eyes legitimate.
You could speak of me in that tone because it's your God
you said to save you from yourself.

I spread my legs for the memory of what once was mine
and the death of it
you pay me
and I pay to remember just one more time
to live a moment longer than disdain.
I am the stain, an ellipsis in the conversation of time and history
so you count me out.
I am your debauchery
the shame in your false dignity
because you will not know me
my body broken into industry
I am just a figment in this history.

Thinner than skin,
whiter than bone,
My children no longer remember their home.
They aspire to other tongues and attitudes
and insult with their newfound platitudes.
Parents who cannot quicken their gaze and raze
this history
remember me
proud Africa is what I used to be.

About AIDS
(for the innocent children who die)

Where she walked the trees fell still
and we played deaf-mute games
while the hunger in her grew
words strangled under the wire pen of this sentence.

It was a dream moaning hard
twilight tunes to the sleepless air.
It was a dream staring back at us there.

Too late for reason
Too late for sorry
Reason figured sullen grace not being the key note in the resonance of this
occupant
HIV an anomaly to a innocence
tainted blood legacy.
inheritance
mother and father to child.

A broken heart
an end before the start,
it drummed its fingers carelessly on the back of her bony skeleton.

In this soliloquy
this occupant closer to her than her jugular
took less from her than you or I.

Jewelled fingerprints

Jewelled fingerprints etch my skin
and the three sisters stare down to mark the time.
We are dreaming,
dreaming stolen lives in the rancour of traffic.
We stuff poster pleasure between on-days,
pods break earth's Psoriasis
slathering coloured paints on lurid air
and sometimes the canvass inhales the quality
a palatable meal these dying memories of beauty in the world.

We are forgotten.
Only in our dreams do we remember ourselves
but they are only dreams and dream-shoes
have no place in a world gone mad.

Psychology and psychiatry frame our faces – bad hairdo daze.
We show the world our possessions; tailored creams on dressers,
  mornings eaten
at a beach somewhere,
our eyes gouged out by an imagined 'what is'
and time and time again
when dark makes me slither between my pores
the jewels of my own fingerprints wake me
and I discover a million journeying in me
that do not belong to this stain we call living.

I disdain to be a part of it, Psoriasis of earth
burrowing like leeches for my own blood.
I sketch my scream onto a faint dawn
and ask myself again why I persist
  when my temper strains at this noose with callous reason.

Far better to die than to watch you kill me with virulent passion.

Island

If we all sat here and drank of our desires and our cravings
and the rubber-muscle courage of drink wrapped itself around us
vice-like
and the lips of our side-splitting laughter whisper soft, sweet nothings
into our ever wanting, ever running, ever hiding hearts,
how long would it take before we unravel splitting sentiment
with the sparkling smiles of our incisors reflecting light from the
chandelier?
There in those luminous, never-empty glasses we expose
the depth of shadows and our little children
little girl, little boy.

Another drink, another line can only make me see more than I desire,
see the craft of my undoing
that shabby rubber-muscle fuck of my undoing.

I am the girl who ran hot and heavy into those arms looking for you,
spreading the vain hope that my heart would be still.
Now that I know the story of love
vain hope, untrue, hopeless,

now my legs have fallen off
and my heart has fallen in on itself and out with itself.
While you gorged on your tongue,
somewhere in my back like a dagger your mother heaved and called,
somewhere in the mist of tongues and kisses,
seething severing limbs

mixing funk and blood and history, you captured me
as you gorged on your tongue and I waited for the right words.
Too late for talk now.
You try to speak bits of words into my lap.
Too late,
only blood will tell a few days from now

you are every man I've ever known.

Where has the girl gone?
(for those who suffer Anorexia)

I don't know if I can touch the palm of your heart with these words.
I don't know how long you've lived away from yourself
there in the neverland of drug-house trauma
and science fiction dulling your voice.
Young girl, it seems you left long ago, so far ago,
so over the world as it grates your spine into shame,
into ruin and plagues of lacquered life.
They sign your name in their outrage and ride your bones
till you clatter
six foot, six foot, six foot.

Sharpened words steal the nature in you away,
looks and hands open you up.
Your mirrors scream at you in horror,
a final nail creeps muscular tendrils all over what was
"Dress so you can please us"
dress for disgust
so you can die small deaths while we practice radiant necrophilia.
Now you're long ago, so far ago
and I cannot reach you though I love you so.

About Rape

I have flowers in my womb,
rough reminders of once upon a time.
I have whispers of beings born and not yet born,
umbilicus ripped and contorted,
distorted into figments of me
all through your blindness
the theft of something you will not understand.

I have Trojan horses milking the illusion of orgasm
so you'll think I'm here.
How you pat yourself on the back, belch satisfaction guaranteed!
And tell the world about the hole in the bed,
the hole in your head.

I have unsaid words throttling the sweet perfume
from my mother and grandmother's tombs.
I have your names and your numbers,
your stench
the putrified remains of your decadence.
I remember you,
a grunting-grating metaphor for making love.

I have flowers in my womb,
invisible to your touch
a cretin's harvest.

About Human

Manvrou, lettie, bulldyke, moffie, stabanie, queer, faggot!
Corrective rape
vain hetero-normative dogma
more right-wing dick mentality dictating the anatomy of my sexuality
my right to be me.

Same sex is shame sex;
is assault with intent to do grievous bodily harm;
is justifiable homicide,
constitutional suicide,
fuck gay pride!
Under the well oiled patriarchal machine
gay and lesbian rights are a distant dream.

Love
is it safe to love her
touch my lover?
My dreams are simple dreams.
They're drink-you-in, smell-your-scent-on-my-skin dreams
yet eyes tell me that this cannot be my reality,
that my dreams are not like yours centred in normality.

I am sick and tired of right wings and left wings that don't fly
when all around I see yet another lie.
Too many of my brothers and sisters waiting to be heard
without the heterosexual configuration that makes their lives an alienation
in a world of sexual bigotry

where I dream democracy is dead.
Here in its place an unchecked hypocrisy lives instead
and legislation makes mockery of emancipation.

I am a gay man
not straight.
This line is crooked like crook,
object crime.
It is criminal you see to be free and to love if you're me.

This is not contained in law, there is no law that vilifies my sexuality.
This law lives in the hearts and minds of those who lead my church
my country.
It lives inside those who share my streets, buses, trains,
my bed
you leave under the skin of night because light would shame the hours
before.

I am sick and tired of the religious remedy
prescribed to me by God-fearing folk
who fear that their carefully constructed reality
may not be all it's made out to be.
Some internal scrutiny may be necessary.
I am by this localised definition of what and how to love
and just who you can love
not free to be part of the same humanity.

Tell me where do we go from here?
We have that sacred cow,
a new constitution in need of execution.
How do we take my body and make it whole again
so I don't have to divide myself between my mother's gaze
and my lover's praise
or my father's shame and my own pain?

How can I simply be a man without the gay
a woman without the lesbian
a human without the question?

Stone words

These are my stones,
hard and thankless baggage bending even the strongest spine.
These are my stones,
they have names like anger, fear, hatred, kill, abuse, alcoholic, suicide.
These are my stones,
they go by other names too:
forgiveness, faith, trust, love, friendship, compassion, respect.
These are my stones,
I have chosen them with care.

So hard are my teachers that they lay their hands on me soft as God's
fingers.
So hard are my teachers that they turn me over and over
till I learn the things I do not want to.
So hard are my teachers that they bend me till I let go into myself and find
God there.

These are my stones and we rub against each other
till my blood paints words on them
and my words paint memory on them.
These are my stones,
they weep, they speak, they live, they laugh
and they love me
till I do.

A song from the egg

River mouths speak of dreams that crash into these seas,
bodies that verge and cluster on a bankrupt shore.
There's a frantic whispering and urgent confusion
banked on the current of a new tribe
as pounding of flesh and pounding of spirit
hide words, hide smiles, hide smells of mother's seasons;
hide songs and truth games in secret places
where ignorance cannot move.

The language of silence grows.
I eat the whips of dissention,
I chew the brute that parts the holy insides of me
for he cannot drown me
he cannot drown me
he cannot drown me
he cannot drown me.

I am coming, can you hear me
can you hear me?
I am coming
I am mending
I am cleaning.
I am casting colours in this space,
learning how to love this face.
I am coming, can you hear me
can you hear me?
I am coming.

I am climbing in your heart
I am shifting in your folds
I am spilling in your seed
I am coming, can you hear me
can you hear me?
I am coming.

I am dreaming in your memory
I am dancing in your shoes
I am breathing in your walk
I am coming can you hear me,
can you hear me?
I am coming.

I am losing feet to become,
losing time to become
losing all to become.

I have woken to my nightmares
I have tangled with my woes
I have begged inside the tomb
I am coming, can you hear me
can you hear me?
I am coming.

My eggshell cracks against your wall,
I hold a mirror to the fall.
I am coming
can you hear me,
can you hear me?
I am
coming.

Home

I have to draw maps.
I have to ride my feet like chariots.
I have to speak like stone and rock.
I have to see like water.
I have to love like mother tongue.
I have to wrestle with the bones of my dead.
I have to wade through the sands, leap through the dungeons
so I feel,
so I feel as I wonder through my life
not knowing me, not knowing now.
See my mirrors and my footprints dance,
me my back to the wind posing in the cracks of my winded smile.
See my questions barren, black shoving marks against these walls,
burning holes in charcoal dreams.
I am here but seldom seen.
I am here,
I am.

I have to draw maps.
I have to ride my feet like chariots.
I have to speak like stone and rock.
I have to see like water.
I have to love like mother tongue.
I have to wrestle with the bones of my dead.
I have to wade through the sands, leap through the dungeons.
so I know,
so I know the dust-stamp footfall,
a murmuring earth call,
knowing where, knowing how
knowing me, knowing now.

I have to draw maps
to make the swindler mute
to sound the horn
to speak by using my own tongue and annihilate the mutant words.

I have to ride my feet like chariots
to win her back
to find her soles and grow my own
in the new places I call home.

I have to wrestle with the bones of my dead
so I may live here in their stead
carrying their wisdom on the lean road
learning the lessons by which I am lead.

I have to wade through the sands,
leap through the dungeons
to find her footprint, to find her footprint
to make a footprint
to make a footprint of my own
so I will know
that I am
home.

Love around midnight

Part 1

The lady's words strum,
she stirs the hum,
she talks to me skating round the apple tree
"Flying too close to the sun child, it's all just fun child?"

That man he sweeps me off my feet
I follow his beat.
His mouth sucks deep from the breath I keep.
I'm not a spider's child,
I don't kill my loving ride
instead I let him
inside.

He touch
I groan
I'm not going home alone.
He says 'I love yous'
he bends my spine.
I sip his wine
he touch
I groan
I'm not going home alone.
The man's hands sing
his music's all on my skin.
I call for God,
I call: "Oh Jesus Lord!"
that man he struck my chord.
He comes
I cry.
All those 'I love yous' die.
He bent my spine
I sipped his wine

the morning came
the sun she rose again
and me
I'll never be the same.

Part 2

My mother never told me nothing 'bout this,
never did.
As you ride my ship
I swear I hear the crack of a heart.
You breathe deep
you go fast
you go slow
you talk more than you know.
We moan high
we moan low
we make the room shake so.
How much of want we know
You're the swizzle stick in my drink,
God if you only know what else I think.
You say please
I say no
you say come
I say go
you say more
I say show.
What in the world do we know?
As we batter the blue night
as we circle the day light
as we hide in the moonlight
as we love
around midnight
turning burn into cold sweat

turning casual into can't get
we pray our hearts won't catch up yet
we pray our hearts won't catch up yet
while we lie soaked in this fishnet.

My mother never told me nothing 'bout this, never did
'bout this midnight
moonlight sweat
caught hard in a fishnet.

Sleeping beauty

You tampered here,
slipping flowers into our hair, tumbling in grasses.
You tampered here
and you grew tits
then lent your walk to hungry eyes,
spilt you cream on indecisive bed sheets.
I lip-read from your words stops and starts of a restless, heady woman
sucking life too fast onto her empty pages.
I lip-read that beneath your easy banter
bravado mosaic
your insanity blinks at me.
You melt rough unfinished tears with intellect.
You play that game
the game of a woman leaning too hard on a porcupine,
grave metaphor and red wine
cigarette smoke and Freud.
You mess your syntax about the table
and feign another fatal attraction
another connection
trying to find a dream of you in a role played too soon
now too long
sheets of ice wake you
unmake you
then break you
as you hurry through your senses
dilated by your fear
another theory
another face
and you grow weary
you see the game.

Princes

I believed you my princes
though I share particles with the wounded
as you dug out bone and flesh to unearth my heart.
I was told always to be careful
because princes are fluent liars
but as I had not learned that language too well
nor understood its culture
I chose belief.

You swiped the morsels of gland and artery round my heart
 and held the organ aloft
to greet the stars
while my brain swooned in its peptic neurosis
and I travelled in under your mountain
sniffing scarcely used paths
while you ate
"Flesh is just flesh," I thought, "what the mountain creature has to say
is the ache in my hunger."
I believed, deaf and blind.
I took my eyes and my ears to beyond and lost the train of conversation
above
so I did not see you swallow hard the bloody syrup of my unerring muscle
and turn on your heel and walk away.

In-fantasy

I am in my infancy troubled to the ship of my stumble and tumble
as I attempt to crawl out of myself onto two legs.
I am in my infancy
growing older as we speak with repetition
the duplication of something I neither believe nor remember – being happy
your face could be that face, their faces, her face or his face
could be
these emotions happened then, with them, with her, with him
they happened.
I spend them
waiting for someone to be original.
I become lavish, sometimes frugal
yet always watching for some sign of difference
a sign of quiet courage.
It never happens
so my infant, vulnerable
almost gladly so
almost always so
sleeps after such analysis.
I have not learned not to cry anymore
yet I have learned to cry differently
resigned, no reassigned
to a magnanimous twist of the mouth I cannot afford.
The currency with which I am charged needs immersion
yet the two-legged fox with the mark-me stare won't dare go there
not all the way.
My tongue supple and muscular talks me into things
verges on speaking too many truths about me
verges on removing the fur on my back
and I am seduced by it
want to undress
want to undo myself on the floor before you
sweet relief to be back I think
but I take my prescription and move along
glancing back so
ever so
often.

A story-poem of imperfection

Pain again
sloth in the fermentation
mud in the water
borrowed looks in the sympathy
broken down words
the precipitation of an old end
an old beginning
one begun a million times without this
without you
without the gnawing enigma of a love that was never really there.
I never quite understood that I was more than this,
more than this strange born-sad woman.
Yes, I feel like I was born sad.

Pain again
never the same again
this is the last time for the shame of the sad mad woman
and fork tongue of spite that mills in those smiles at the dead of night.
Pain again
though not the same again,
the scent of change is slight yet remains.

To be honest, one grows accustomed to the presence of this sharpness
this trickle of acid in the veins.
It's a drug, a mate
the mask on the shoulder of spite.
Oh spite, the star to the undeserved
and the swift whip in the hand of judgement.

Pain again
not like before.
There's a faint glimmer of hope knocking at my door
the roll of a hum
the twist of a seed in the hope of a deed so small
that it becomes the hardest of all
one with no flash and no witness or fame
one that determines the depth of sorrow or smile

one that names my body a shell
so small that it becomes the hardest of all
to love oneself.

These seeds of deception clone dark thoughts,
they resurrect the taunt of children
the memory of that which is half dead
"There are many people skirting the backstreets of disaster
while you're sitting here thinking of the many ways to die,"
she said to me once.
Never mind, I knew she meant well
but you see the ecstasy of guilt
has an arrow swifter than your disgust.
If you know then you should know this:
guilt is the consummate artist of deception like no other
swifter than your disgust I tell you
is the whip in my hand beating abuse
like a metronome.

The twist of a seed
in the hope of a deed so small
that it becomes the hardest of all
to love oneself.

Noisier than a prism screeching its light
I am screaming snake-fire into crust and rouge
"No more!" I scream, "No more!"
as you fire snake-fire into my orchestra
with the yellow moonlight serenade tongue
of that song you keep singing while I sleep my 'she' hypnosis.
You pounce song there while the bones of my courage look the other way.
Shame, is that the only way you love me?
When I am down?
When I am a shadow cursed with an old rag, "Now," you say,
"Now I can love you!"
You love a dead story.
You love me when I'm gone, when I am breeching the seams of my soul.

You love me when I sell myself.
Oh lover, I am screaming snake-fire into crust and rouge,
I am a river in flood weeping the taste of my sins as they depart
and twist and turn one more time to kiss me hard.
I drunk on those angry passions of yours
I drunk on your mother's sins
by your father's crimes.
I am where you are not.
We both love another
a haunting her and a hunting there.
Chasing the tail of a dragon we fall on the spear, twist on the wire
false lips resurrect the same old game.
Oh lover, such a sad, tired, almost over- lying shame.

The twist of a seed
in the hope of a deed so small that it becomes the hardest of all
to love oneself when you stumble and fall,
the hardest one of all.

A love poem for Africa

We could dance a moment,
kiss the ground with urgent feet
that spell our names for the moon and the sun.
Is your heart in your soles like mine
rumbling thick like heart in Feb
tracing its pulse in the red dust
shedding cloud in the musk of night.

I'm sipping on your black
smothered in colour brighter than light.
We could dance a moment
one shadow thick like heat smothered in black
colour brighter than light.

We could dance a moment.
My spine grows swollen with wanting feet.
The sleep in my labyrinth smells you at a loud distance.
The tree of this tale grows deep in the ground
wearing roots like a vapour.

I'm sipping on your black
smothered in colour brighter than light.

We could dance a moment.
I feel the salt of that motion dry on my tongue.
I have no edge
no end
I'm mad on the wicked smoke of your skin.

I'm sipping on your black
smothered in colour brighter than light
brighter than light
brighter than light
than light
than light
than light
light.

Surrender

This is my surrender to my body shape
the thigh to which I refer only with grimace and malcontent
the plump slope of matter at my rear
that has been the cause of so much discontent
so much embarrassment
to this end I now repent
to this house of that enigmatic entity the soul
to this tower of flagellation, diet probations
the foundation of an industry that has belittled me
I surrender much of my own distaste.

In this attitude I have misplaced my dignity, my self-esteem
and too many a romantic dream
misguided by the idea that the rule for body shape
is somehow trapped in the
mono-slope
the one handful grope
the thirty, thirty-two if you stand next to me no one will see you
we're talking side- view dream
buy yourself that exercise machine, melt away the kilojoules
to please these maniacal
fools
who are filling their wallets while we're masticating lettuce leaves
riveted by an unattainable pedigree to satisfy visually.

Well what about touch?
More than you can manage?
More than you can wrap your mind around?
That I get
hypnotised, bought and taught to deny ourselves this kind of delight
the experience of the voluptuous
captured and recaptured by the old masters who identified child bearing
hips
or simply being healthy as beautiful.

The canon the silhouette
sadly one of the many subplots to the face of femicide
"Keep the queen in her cage!"
and while we're here what about anorexia and bulimia?
Suicide princesses
a rough ride through what I like to call image cuisine
getting women to hate themselves!
An internalised oppression case study.

My sisters, where are we really when we let them fill us up
with more self-deprecating notions
on this nurtured human family tree?
Fuck that!
Today I surrender myself completely to this body shape
understanding finally what a privilege it is to be
all of me.

Men-on-pause

I could cogitate, masturbate
get a tax rebate, fraternise with yet another ingrate
or possibly negotiate
the relativity of love in my mid-life heightened sexual state
but which country is that in?
Do you know?
So many instruments for diverse one- person pleasure fly to mind
but hands and lips and tongue push through
and the fingered need of take one
postulates in the silence
like a period.

Where have all the men gone?
The ones who can dive in, dig up
throw my body into backbend and somersault
and catapult me into songs that mimic some favoured operatic aria.
I am in Siberia
melting ice with my mental ejaculations on who to conjure up next.
I am the creator of my universe after all.

Perhaps I should learn yoga
and meditate or levitate
conspire with other witches and cast spells to attract a mate
or sell my produce at the nearest bar
but been there
done that
so now what?

Is there a better man than me out there?
One with balls enough to say: "Let's make it a date each, say, Saturday"
to bounce the headboard off the wall
let the neighbours know we've had it all
burn our shins on the carpet in the hall
and baste the sheets with orgasm and more-gasm
and then start all over again
but the lust to run it seems is more fun than a role in the hay

so I pull down my panties
while my cupboard stares back at my crack
and I switch on my humming vibrator
whom I've affectionately named Jack
at least I know next Saturday
he'll be back.

Short legs, long road home

Short legs, chafing thighs with the sun in my three-years-old
vineyard colours, barbed wire fences and farmers
threatening to shoot naughty little children hungry for the taste of grape
and drama.
Plum trees and ghosts waiting outside,
milk breasts and wheelchair archers
regal with emblazoned bottle-green jackets,
wall-to-wall graffiti
and three storeys in spaces to small for you and me,
little boys calling across balconies,
men on street corners lighting pipes
to save themselves
from living.

I don't know where I come from sometimes –
somewhere, where the Khoi never sang
Peaches and Herb, Ramsey Lewis and Earth, Wind and Fire
on a Sunday,
marigold, dahlia, sweetpea,
white- liver legs watering our garden,
women loud and raunchy saying and doing the things
other women frown at,
old men leering at little girls twisting like ripe fruit
across sounds half grown-up and too young still,

Streets of stone,
bottleneck castaways followed by Old Brown sherry Fridays for us,
first thing you spent your wages on that day right?
From wanting to be heard to no beginning
where you and I and people I don't know live
in slave ritual.

These odd memories are gooseflesh sounds under my skin
like metal blade signature man to man in Algoa court and Ambrose
crescent,
yet what did I know about these things,
still my mother's child caught on her nurse's uniform leash?

But I learned,
I learned of dead-ends and cigarettes sooner than sunset;
I learned of aching in places under my clothes
more hidden than illusion;
I learned men too soon;
learned colour and geography and shame;
I learned to say yes when I meant no;
learned to accept blame even though I was not responsible;
learned to squeeze myself into tight corners
so you'd never find me there in your way.

The nostalgic wind only smelt of illusion
and these tears only taste of sadness – wish it were true.
Such things are never spoken of,
all ears are deaf
and all mouths are busy with the business of making noise
and losing memory
but nobody's busy with feeling and dealing
and the eyes,
the eyes trace your invisibility without remorse;
the eyes turn over back into their socket
the shadows of rainbows in them;
the eyes are not seeing instruments.

There are tender places
where once I hoped that you would come to the mirror with me,
brittle ends to my dreams
yet I have sweetened them
with the words
to my new "once upon a time."

OTHER POETRY TITLES BY MODJAJI BOOKS

Fourth Child by Megan Hall
Life in Translation by Azila Talit Reisenberger
Please, Take Photographs by Sindiwe Magona
Burnt Offering by Joan Metelerkamp
Strange Fruit by Helen Moffett
Oleander by Fiona Zerbst
The Everyday Wife by Phillippa Yaa de Villiers
missing by Beverly Rycroft
These are the lies I told you by Kerry Hammerton
Conduit by Sarah Frost
The Suitable Girl by Michelle McGrane
Piece Work by Ingrid Andersen
Difficult Gifts by Dawn Garisch
Woman Unfolding by Jenna Mervis
removing by Melissa Butler
At least the Duck Survived by Margaret Clough
Bare & Breaking by Karin Schimke
The Reckless Sleeper by Haidee Kruger